THE VIEW
FROM
MY HEART

THE VIEW
FROM
MY HEART

LaJean Wilson

Pleasant W rd

Pleasant Word (a division of WinePress Publishing, PO Box 428, Enumclaw, WA 98022) functions only as book publisher. As such, the ultimate design, content, editorial accuracy, and views expressed or implied in this work are those of the author.

The author of this book has waived the publisher's suggested editing and proof reading services. As such, the author is responsible for any errors found in this finished product.

Unless otherwise noted, all Scriptures are taken from the *Holy Bible, New International Version*®, NIV®. Copyright © 1973, 1978, 1984 by the International Bible Society. Used by permission of Zondervan. All rights reserved.

Scriptures marked NKJV are taken from the Holy Bible, New King James Version, Copyright 1982 by Thomas Nelson, Inc.

ISBN 13: 978-1-4141-1058-5
ISBN 10: 1-4141-1058-8
Library of Congress Catalog Card Number: 2007904997

DEDICATION

This book is dedicated to my husband, Chuck, who has always encouraged me to shoot for the stars. He believes in me and constantly lets me know that he thinks I can do anything. His compassion for others inspires me every day. I am blessed to be his wife.

TABLE OF CONTENTS

Foreword ix

FAMILY

Chapter One: The Change Motherhood Makes 15
Chapter Two: The More Important 19
Chapter Three: A New Name for a New Role 23
Chapter Four: A Year of Lasts 27
Chapter Five: A Legacy of Words.............................. 31

MARRIAGE

Chapter Six: A Testimony of God's Grace 37
Chapter Seven: Marriage 101 ..,............................... 39

HOLIDAYS

Chapter Eight: Love in the Air 45
Chapter Nine: The Hope That Was Born 49
Chapter Ten: Thankful for Tears 53

Chapter Eleven: The Glass Half-full............................ 57
Chapter Twelve: It's a Wonderful Life 61
Chapter Thirteen: Not a Fruitcake, but a Nut 65
Chapter Fourteen: My Christmas Heritage 69
Chapter Fifteen: A New Year Scrooge 75

FRIENDSHIP

Chapter Sixteen: The Stuff of Life 81
Chapter Seventeen: Gold Friends 85
Chapter Eighteen: Stranded: Miracles on
    the Pinnacle 89

SEASONS OF LIFE

Chapter Nineteen: Do I Look Like a Hillbilly? 97
Chapter Twenty: The Pain of Letting Go 103
Chapter Twenty-One: The Empty Nest 107
Chapter Twenty-Two: A Temporary Residence 111

TRAVEL

Chapter Twenty-Three: Expecting the Good 117
Chapter Twenty-Four: A Helicopter Prayer 121
Chapter Twenty-Five: The Older, the Better 125
Chapter Twenty-Six: Traveling Light........................ 129

Epilogue 133
Endnotes 135

FOREWORD

For me it's all about the view. If we go to the beach, we must have a view of the ocean. If we go to the mountains, I'd better be able to see an entire mountain range from my windows. The first thing I do in a city hotel is open the curtains to see if we have a spectacular view of the city from our room. I totally understand charging more for a New York City hotel room because it overlooks Central Park. So naturally I decided that this book is really all about the view–not just the view as I see it outside through my windows but the view as I see it from inside my mind. This book is nothing more than a commentary on the views of life I've had in the past few years–the simple everyday experiences of watching the world change around me. It's about the view I see with my heart, not my eyes.

Heart has always been an important word for me as well. For several years I was a part of a great group of women in our church who met for Bible Study every week and named our group *Heartwarming*. Later, for several years I edited and wrote a column for a local magazine called *Good News*. My column was naturally called "From the **Heart** of the Editor." That column became the basis for this book. In each issue I just basically wrote about whatever topic was going through my head (or touching my heart) at the time. It was a terrific luxury and great therapy–having an outlet to express my views from my heart every month, with no editing from anyone else. Having all of these personal essays already written, I thought, "What an easy way to write a book!" I'm sorry if you thought I just spent the last five years laboring over the creation of this book; if it's intellectual and cerebral stimulation you're looking for, this is not it. It's just a lazy way to write a book.

I need to say *thank you* to a few people. Well, I actually need to say *thank you* to a lot of people, but I'm afraid I'll forget somebody. So I'll just say, "You know who you are." I'll just simply thank my family, my extended family, my church family (at Russellville First Free Will Baptist Church), my friends, my teachers, my mentors, and my colleagues. I think that about covers it. Chuck, Chip, and CaraJean–you are the wind beneath my wings, the lights of my life, the…every other cliché I can think of. Seriously, you three know that you have given me the two roles in life that I love the most–wife and mother–and you have given me indescribable joy and love (and fun) in those roles. Alison, thank you for loving Chip, and Matt, thank you for loving CaraJean. Mom and Dad, thank you for always believing that I could do anything and for loving all of your children unconditionally.

Most of all, thank you, God, for blessing me with these.

FAMILY

CHAPTER ONE

THE CHANGE MOTHERHOOD MAKES

Just three days after Mother's Day this year my firstborn child graduated from high school. This was a lethal combination for a sentimental softie like me. If you saw me during that week, you probably offered me a Kleenex. My baby boy is now a full-grown man, and somehow this happened in just a short eighteen years that seems more like eighteen months. The changes from babyhood to boyhood to manhood that take place during those years are swift and obvious. Looks change, clothes are outgrown, voices change–so many things seem to just change overnight. But what about me–the mother of that child? Did I grow up? I can't possibly be old enough to be the mother of an adult, can I? Yes, I can, and I am. But how have I changed?

To say becoming a mother changes one's life would be a drastic understatement, like saying that the Titanic was a boat that had an accident. Someone once said, "Being a mother is like having a part of your heart walking around outside your body." So true. I could never have imagined how far your heart could stretch. That inexpressible love, the enormity of the responsibility of that little life, and the overwhelming emotions of motherhood engulfed me during those first few months as a mother. I found myself in a whole new world. Instead of conversing with my colleagues in the world of academia about classic works of literature, I spent most of my days as a stay-at-home mom using unintelligible one-word sentences all day. But that was okay; I couldn't help myself. I loved baby talk. Actually I quite preferred hearing my child's voice and attempt at words and sentences to the voice of any great orator or speaker. Mothers understand this–baby babble is the most precious sound in the world. But I would have never understood that before; motherhood had changed me.

As for books, I quickly forgot about the classics or the best-sellers of the day. Picture books were much more fun. Mother Goose and Dr. Seuss were the big hits at my house, along with books like *The Little Engine That Could.* I found that a simple little picture book called *Love You Forever* could (and still does) cause me to sob every time I read it. It's just another one of those "mother things."

Even though I had never played any sports in my life (I was never athletic in any sense of the word) and knew very little about sports, I suddenly became interested in sports as soon as Chip reached Little League age. As a matter of fact, I became an expert on sports of all kinds, at least enough of an expert to yell and scream right along with the rest of the parents. One day when I actually heard my mild-mannered, quiet, and meek self standing and yelling at a bad call at a basketball game, I realized that I had become one of those obnoxious parents I was sure that I'd never be. But things were different now. My son was out there playing football, basketball, and baseball. I was not only interested; I was a fan! I have spent a good part of the last eighteen years sitting on bleachers (especially since my second child is an athlete, also). I have screamed, yelled, and cheered. Trust me—this is not my personality, but motherhood has changed everything. I became a competitive person where my children were concerned. Mothers also understand this principle: you may hurt my feelings, but you'd better not even think about hurting my child's feelings! Yet I've weathered those things, too, during the years. I've had to deal with the inevitable broken heart that comes with adolescence and those tumultuous teen years, and I have survived.

Yes, I have changed over the eighteen years that I've been a mother. I can be over-protective, over-bearing, competitive, overly sentimental, and yes, sometimes I'm tired and I feel old. But I have also learned to love unconditionally, to give when I'm too tired to give, to reach beyond myself, to stretch and grow, and to experience in a very small way what great love the Father had for us as He gave up His only Son to die for us. When I realize how much I love my children, I realize what a great sacrifice He made in giving up the Son He so loved.

We are told in the Psalms that children are a gift of the Lord. I'm so thankful for that precious gift. And I still quote one of my favorite literary classics to my big grown-up son:

> *I'll love you forever. I'll like you for always.*
> *As long as I'm living, my baby you'll be.*

> *Sons are a heritage from the Lord, children a*
> *reward from him.*
> —Psalm 127:3

CHAPTER TWO

THE MORE IMPORTANT

It was about three weeks before the wedding. Our son had come home to "clean out" his room. Even though he had been living in his own apartment for about a year and a half, his room still looked pretty much the same as it did before he left. Now he was spending the day organizing, sorting, packing boxes, and still leaving stacks of mementos in his closet.

Late that night I couldn't sleep, so I wandered into his room and looked around. The walls were blank; the desk was empty; the floor was clear. It was hard to choke back the tears at the sight of the barren room. It seemed like only yesterday that we had added to our house a new bedroom and bathroom for Chip–then a still-growing but already over six feet tall freshman in high school who literally had outgrown his old room. How quickly that time had passed! As I looked around, something caught my eye–the wallpaper border in the bathroom. When we had built the room, the painter had put a wallpaper border around the bedroom. Later I decided that even I, totally inept at that sort of thing, could surely put the same border up in the tiny bathroom. I did manage to put part of it up; but then I became frustrated with the whole thing and just stopped where I was, fully intending to finish it someday soon. Now I noticed that the wallpaper border had never been finished. "Wait!" I wanted to scream. "We've got to rewind time just a little bit! I've left things unfinished. Maybe there are other things I didn't finish, left undone, or never said. He can't already be getting married and leaving home when I haven't even finished his room yet!"

But it was true that he had grown up and left home, and I thought about all of the things that I wished I had done. But maybe, just maybe, I left some things undone because there were more important things to do. Maybe I didn't finish the wallpaper because I went to all of his ballgames and attended his activities at school and helped him with this homework. Maybe I didn't ever get his room organized or his scrapbooks put together because I listened to him tell me about his day, or about his hopes and dreams, or about his disappointments. Maybe it was okay that I had left some things undone, as long as I had traded them for the more important.

I felt better. The room was still too quiet; the walls were still too bare; the shelves were still too neat. But the memories of those important, intangible things in life–love, laughter, relationship–have a way of filling an empty room, or even an aching heart.

> *But Mary treasured up all these things and*
> *pondered them in her heart.*
> —Luke 2:19

CHAPTER THREE

A NEW NAME FOR A NEW ROLE

I am about to assume a new role in life. I've had quite a few. I've been a daughter and sister and cousin and niece and aunt. For over twenty-five years I've been a wife, and for the last twenty-one years I've been a mother. I've been a teacher, a business owner, an editor, and a publisher. But I will now become the most maligned (although unfairly so) woman in this country–I will be the mother-in-law, the object of multitudes of jokes, all unflattering. Have you ever heard a father-in-law joke? I didn't think so. I haven't. Only the ever-present mother-in-law joke. On the television and movie screen and in print, mothers-in-law are always portrayed as interfering, annoying, nosy, critical, whining, emotionally unreasonable, and downright tacky. Of course I plan to be the antithesis of such a mother-in-law with just the right balance of offering only loving support, minding my own business, and only giving advice when asked. I will never interfere, annoy, or criticize. Don't laugh. I'm trying to start a new image and break out of the old stereotype.

Mother's Day is an important day in the month of May, but I say, "Mothers-in-law of the world, unite!" It's our turn to have a day. Of course, all mothers-in-law are already mothers, but I don't see why we shouldn't have two different days in our honor. After all, we have accomplished two amazing feats. First, we have brought children into the world and raised them through the sometimes difficult and always challenging years. Then, after we have done all of the hard part and have gone through grueling years of work in turning them into normal, well-adjusted (for the most part) adult human beings, we give them to someone else. Is that fair?

So, let's outlaw the word "in-law" and call ourselves something else. Let's ban mother-in-law jokes, or at least demand equal time for father-in-law jokes.

Chip and Alison, you know I love you and want only the best for you. And I promise to do the best I can to be a good mother-in-law. But, Alison, the first time I forget to mind my own business and run the risk of becoming the dreaded stereotypical joke, please remind me of these words I've written. And, by the way, I have some things for you to read with good words of advice on marriage…uh, oh….that sounded like a mother-in-law, didn't it?

…then Orpah kissed her mother-in-law good-by,
but Ruth clung to her.
—Ruth 1:14

CHAPTER FOUR

A YEAR OF LASTS

Those who know me well know I always have a "sappy" story to tell about my kids. Today is no exception. You see, it's been an emotional two months for me. The tears have come often and profusely, so indulge me as I reminisce. In these few weeks our oldest child got married, my parents celebrated their fiftieth wedding anniversary (with a big sentimental reception with family and friends), and our youngest child had her Senior pictures made in order to get a head start on her upcoming busy Senior year.

Family ties, traditions, and the passing on of a heritage from generation to generation have never been more meaningful to me. My parents have not only been married for fifty years, but they have been happily married in a loving, nurturing home for their five very fortunate children (me, Frank, Lisa, Sheila, and Kim–in that order). I'm so glad that my children have had the privilege of growing up in the circle of their grandparents' influence. My dad, who is a minister, performed my son's wedding ceremony. As he talked to them about establishing a Christian home, he reminded them of the scriptural admonition in Deuteronomy. "Teach them (God's words) to your children, talking about them when you sit at home and when you walk along the road, when you lie down, and when you get up." I know that as he spoke those words, my children realized that their grandparents have been living those words for fifty years. Dad's words were not just words; they were alive, a living legacy from his example.

But now, the season of weddings, reunions, and vacations has given way to the season of books, school, work, and frantic activity. The coming of fall can mean only one thing this year–my baby, that sweet little angel who started kindergarten just last year (or so it seems), is a Senior!! It's the last year I'll have a child in school (other than college). This will be a year of "lasts"–the last first day of school, the last chance to get that "first day of school" picture she loves so much (yeah, right!), the last season-opener ball game, the last Homecoming, the last…well, you get the picture. I guess it's best I stop now. I need to go to the store anyway. I'll have to get another case of Kleenex.

A good man leaves an inheritance for his children's children...
—Proverbs 13:22a

CHAPTER FIVE

A Legacy of Words

After writing a magazine column for about six years, I was running out of things to say. I had rambled about my marriage, my children, my travels, our holiday celebrations, and my opinions in general. I had told everyone more than they wanted to know about my life at times. Maybe I had fallen into a rut. Maybe I had a writer's block. Maybe my empty nest did not provide me with the stories that are a natural part of a full one. I even thought that maybe I needed to pray for something exciting, funny, touching, or newsworthy to happen to me to give me new material. On second thought, maybe that wasn't a good idea. There is something to be said for a relatively uneventful time of peace and quiet and the simple life because we can be fairly sure that it won't last.

I was writing for a May/June issue at the time, so I thought maybe I'd do something for Mother's Day and Father's Day. I thought about how thankful I was for my parents and the love, support, and teaching that they had given me. They have taught my siblings and me so much, not just with words, but by their example. They are the best examples of Godly parents that I know. I am blessed more than I can express.

Actually, I believe that one thing my parents gave me was a love for the written word. My mother not only loves to read, but she loves to write as well. Much of her writing is in the form of poetry. Through the years she has written many letters of love and encouragement to her children (even when we were still at home) that contained "words fitly spoken" in lines that rhymed.

My dad, who also loves to read, is a preacher who is a master storyteller. He does most of his storytelling in the form of the spoken word. He is the definition of the term "people person"–he can always find someone with whom to share his stories and his sense of humor. He not only has wonderful stories to tell from his own life, but he has been handed down some amazing true stories from the lives of his family members from generations past. He has promised me that he is beginning to write some of them down; I hope he does. Writing or recording his own telling of many of these stories will be a treasured inheritance for future generations to enjoy.

After thinking through these things, I somehow began to feel a little more inspired to write again. Maybe the writer's block wouldn't last long after all. I knew it all along–my parents always were an inspiration to me. Thanks, Mom and Dad. I love you.

> *A word fitly spoken is like apples of gold in*
> *settings of silver.*
> —Proverbs 25:11 (NKJV)

MARRIAGE

CHAPTER SIX

A TESTIMONY OF GOD'S GRACE

It's true. I've been married twenty-five years. I can't believe it. I don't know if I'm just amazed (that I'm old enough) or proud (it's quite an accomplishment) or just blessed (that God has been so good to us). I guess that's it. Any long-standing marriage (especially a long, **happy** marriage) is a testimony of God's grace. Just the fact that we're both still breathing is a testimony of God's goodness. The fact that we're still married is a testimony of God's blessing. And the fact that we actually still love each other and enjoy each other's company is a testimony of God's mercy. The fact that he is still my best friend and I am his could probably only be classified as a miracle.

We are very different. We argue. We disagree… often. I see the glass half-empty; he sees it half-full.

If I say we should turn left, he will invariably say we should turn right. But we have never disagreed on the important things in life—the life goals that we have as a couple and for our family. We agree on our priorities, on our faith, and on our plans and dreams. We both want to have a ministry for God, and we want to do it together. We both want to travel and see the world, but only if we can do it together.

I was asked recently to do a devotion at a wedding shower, and I thought about all of the things that I would want to tell a young couple starting out on this wonderful adventure called marriage. You can learn a lot in twenty-five years. But you can also learn very little. I see people who seem to be making the same mistakes that they made from the beginning. And if they're even still together, they're miserable. Marriage, just like progress, requires change. Marriages need tending, just like gardens. There are too many weeds along the roads that can choke the life from our relationships.

If you have a happy marriage, thank God for it and realize what a blessing it is. If you don't, seek God's guidance and the counsel of others in how to change things (which very often may mean "God, change **me**"). And always remember…"A happy home is one in which both mates think that they got better than they deserve." I know I did.

He who finds a wife finds what is good and
receives favor from the Lord.
—Proverbs 18:22

CHAPTER SEVEN

MARRIAGE 101

When I was growing up, all of my friends and classmates lived with their moms and dads in the same home. As my children grew up in the same town, less than half of their classmates lived with both mom and dad. I wonder how differently the young adults of today view marriage in light of living their lives surrounded with the reality of divorce. Are they more frightened? Less naïve? More nonchalant about commitment? Or more determined?

I haven't done a comprehensive poll, but the young people with whom I spoke seemed more determined than ever to be sure, to be committed, and to stay married. They don't just assume that marriages always last because they've seen otherwise. An important part of pre-wedding planning for some Christian couples today is the counseling that they receive through the church. One young couple told me of an "expectations" test that they took in their counseling process to see if they had compatible expectations of marriage. I think that many young people do go into marriage expecting something totally unrealistic (such as for their spouses to change) and become disappointed or disillusioned when things aren't quite what they expected. Perhaps our churches are beginning to teach and prepare young couples for this major step—I hope so. Before I was married we had no preparation, no counseling, and no teaching about marriage; we learned the hard way. But we were determined to stay together, and we took it for granted then that marriages were supposed to last—"for better, for worse; 'til *death* do us part."

I have wondered what advice I would have to give young brides and grooms. What would I say to them? What have I learned in thirty-plus years of marriage? What would I say in the classroom of Marriage 101?

First, and this is really profound—marriage means a whole lot of hard work. And I do mean *work*. But you have to balance that work with fun. I read somewhere (unfortunately, I can't remember where) that marriage means Mundane Monday Mornings, but it should also mean moonlight and roses. Marriage means Too-Tired Tuesdays and Fighting Fridays (I like those descriptions!), but marriage should also mean romantic rendezvous and passionate anniversaries. I've learned that marriage means sharing–sharing bills, bathrooms, bad habits, and bleak times. But marriage also means sharing breakfast in bed, the best of times, blessed events, and the blessing of having someone with whom to share all of life's moments.

Marriage is not a 50/50 proposition. It's not, "I'll do my share if he'll do his share." It is a covenant, not a contract. Unless each partner intends to give 100%, regardless of what the other person does, a marriage is crippled from the start. That's total commitment. Spiritual strength comes from knowing that kind of agape love that God has for us, the perfect example of sacrificial love. That's loving no matter what the return may be–loving "**no matter what.**" My husband gave me a card once that said, "Anyone can love when it's easy, but you continue to love even when I make it very difficult. Thanks for loving me no matter what." There will be a lot of "no matter what" times. There will be more mundane Monday mornings and too-tired Tuesdays than there will be moonlight and roses rendezvous. That's why you need those moonlight and roses experiences–they help you to get through the mundane Mondays. Don't wait for special occasions to make special times. Make ordinary occasions special. Be creative. I love the line from a Conrad Aiken poem, "Music I heard with you was more than music, and bread I broke with you was more than bread." Make everyday bread and music extraordinary.

As individuals you will grow and learn, and your marriage will grow and strengthen if you keep sharing all of your growing with each other. Marriage is a living entity–it has to be nurtured. Don't let it become too comfortable or too complacent and eventually stop growing. It's often all too easy to take each other for granted, but don't let that happen.

I have heard it said that in this life it doesn't matter what you have or where you go; what matters is who walks beside you. Keeping that in mind helps you appreciate the gift of having someone with whom to share life's journey, and that gift is one of the best God gives any of us.

My beloved is mine and I am his.
—Song of Solomon 2:16 (NKJV)

HOLIDAYS

CHAPTER EIGHT

LOVE IN THE AIR

It's the month of February, and love is in the air. At least that's what the world of advertising is telling me. It's the month of Valentine's Day, and that means that everywhere you look there are hearts, flowers, candy, cards…well, you've seen it all. Not that I object–I like romance and flowers and jewelry and candy. I really do. And I honestly believe that "love is a many-splendored thing" and "it's what the world needs now" and all of those other song titles. But I think that maybe the word *love* is one of the most overused words in the English language. We use it to mean many different things, and consequently sometimes it doesn't mean much at all. We need more than one word to use to describe how we feel, but if we *really like* something a lot, we just have to say *love*. We love our couch, the color of that dress, your haircut, her chocolate cake, that song. We love our friends, our neighbors, our siblings, our children, our spouses, and, oh yes, our God…all with the same four little letters. But we really don't feel the same about all of those things, do we?

Maybe I just want the word *love* to mean much more than hearts and flowers. It's more than a way to sell candy. Every passage on love in the Bible tells us just how powerful, how meaningful, how committed, how perfect **real** love is. I Corinthians 13:8 says that love never fails. I hate to admit it, but I'm afraid that the earthly love we have for things and even for some people very often fails. The good news is that there is a love that never has and never will fail or even slightly fade—the love of God. It provides us with the model for what the word *love* should mean.

At this moment love **is** in the air in our family. About a year ago my husband and I reached the milestone of our twenty-fifth wedding anniversary. Now we are approaching another milestone. This spring our first-born child is getting married, so we are thinking and talking a lot about wedding "stuff" around our house. It's a sweet time; it's a difficult time. I guess we have reached that time in life when changes in our family are inevitable—that time when our children are graduating from high school, leaving home for college, moving out for good, getting married. That all involves an aspect of love that is very difficult to do, but it's a part of love, nonetheless–letting go. The "root" work has been done; now it's time for the "wings."

> *And now these three remain: faith, hope, and*
> *love. But the greatest of these is love.*
> —I Corinthians 13:13

CHAPTER NINE

THE HOPE THAT WAS BORN

It was early September, and I needed to start thinking about a magazine column I was going to write for the holidays. It was difficult to think of holiday ideas during those warm September days.

Then it happened–that horrible September 11 that none of us will ever forget. For days I stayed glued to the television with a sick feeling in the pit of my stomach, a lump in my throat, and tears in the rims of my eyes. I kept looking for something to make sense–maybe a reason, a meaning, an understanding. I'm not sure I ever found it. But I did see great compassion and courage in the face of grief that I had never before seen in my lifetime. I saw an outpouring of love and caring for fellow human beings. I heard prayers called out loudly to God. I witnessed patriotism and watched heroes at work.

I saw so many good things happening in America that the tears came not only from grief, but also from pride. I saw lawmakers calling on God to help us. I saw our President call for a national prayer service. I saw people praying in public places, and I heard no one complain about it. I saw people giving their time, their money, their services, and yes, even their lives to assist or rescue those in need. It was a remarkable, moving, heart-wrenching few weeks. In the wake of the unbelievably horrific news that we all witnessed, we had surely seen some encouraging good news about our country.

A year earlier I had written a column about the fact that you can find nice, kind people everywhere, even in New York City. I had told about my trips there and how surprised I was to find that the people were not the stereotypical rude, brash, uncaring New Yorkers I had expected to find. Now the whole world had seen the same thing. We were extremely proud of our fellow Americans–and those in New York had given us a good example to follow.

But the time had come to write the holiday article, and things were uncertain at best. We were all wondering about the future while realizing that only God knew what lay ahead. What about the holidays that year? Should we celebrate? Surely Thanksgiving would be a profoundly meaningful holiday for all Americans that year. When we thanked God for America and asked Him to bless her that Thanksgiving, surely we would no longer be giving a mere lip service to our prayers. "God Bless America" was no longer just a song title–it was a fervent prayer of our hearts.

Would we celebrate Christmas as usual that year, or would we hold each moment and each family member closely to our hearts as we remembered how many of our fellow Americans would be missing their loved ones? Would we finally realize that the important things in life must not be taken for granted?

Would there be peace on Christmas? No, there would probably not be peace from a worldly standpoint. But there could be peace in the hearts of those who know the Prince of Peace. Would there be good will toward all men? Not likely. But Christians could show the love and compassion toward others that we had seen demonstrated so vividly in the recent times of tragedy.

Christmas would be difficult for so many that year, but it was important that we as Christians continued to show the world that we still had reason to celebrate. We needed more than ever to celebrate life. We had to show that love is stronger than hate. We still had to show that we had hope–the Hope that was born in a manger at Christmas.

…while we wait for the blessed hope–the glorious
appearing of our great God and Savior,
Jesus Christ.
—Titus 2:13

CHAPTER TEN

THANKFUL FOR TEARS

As Thanksgiving was approaching, I was thinking of my usual "I'm thankful for" list. But I thought of something that we may not always think of in our blessing lists. I am thankful for tears. I have often poked fun at myself about my sentimental nature and my tendency to get emotional over so many nostalgic moments and milestones in life. But, in all seriousness, tears are a blessing to me.

I'm thankful for happy tears, of course, because they are a way to release some of the fullness of joy that wells up inside us sometimes. But I'm also thankful for the emotional release that tears give us in all kinds of situations.

Just a year after 9/11 I had the opportunity to spend a brief three days in New York City. As it turned out, it seemed to be an emotional trip for me. My husband and I visited Ground Zero and walked around the area with hundreds of other people. There were ten thousand firemen from all over the world in the city that weekend to attend a special memorial service being held for all of the firemen who had died on 9/11–yes, even though it had already been a year at that time. I watched as the firemen who were there that day walked around the site. I saw the emotion in their faces and the tears in their eyes, and I couldn't help but feel the tears myself. We walked around and looked at all of the memorials, the lists of those who had died, and the remembrances sent from all over the world. We went inside St. Paul's Chapel, where so many workers and others found solace during the months of recovery and clean-up. I saw the scars, scratches, and marks on the white backs of the beautiful pews where workers had come in with their equipment and had lain down to rest. We were told that the pews are not going to be repainted–the stains and scratches will remain as a reminder and a memorial. We could not sit in that church without feeling the tears come. How many tears of grief and mourning had been shed in that little haven of rest during the long nightmarish months after 9/11?

On the same night we took a two-hour cruise in the harbor around the island of Manhattan and saw the Statue of Liberty, lit up at night in all of its majesty. Its beauty could take your breath away. It was a sight that surely no American could see without a lump forming in his or her throat. I know it did in mine, and the tears of patriotism and pride filled my eyes.

We also had the privilege of attending a service at the Brooklyn Tabernacle and listening to that choir sing–tears of joy just could not contain that awesome experience. It's hard to explain what a moving expression of worship those songs were. There is nothing like being there and hearing that choir live.

Yes, it sounds as if I just cried all during that trip, but they were good tears. Even the tears of grief and mourning provide such an outlet for our emotions that they give us a needed release. And tears of pride and joy–well, sometimes we just need a way to exhale all that makes our hearts feel as if they will surely burst. As I've heard others say, "When my cup overflows, it comes out my eyes."

Because we all have different emotional patterns and personalities, we don't all express our emotions in the same way. Some people just simply do not cry as easily as others do, and that's perfectly okay. I happen to be one of those people who sometimes know that we'll probably feel better if we can just "have a good cry!"

I am reminded of the familiar words of Ecclesiastes 3: "There is a time for everything, and a season for every activity under heaven…a time to weep and a time to laugh, a time to mourn and a time to dance…a time to be silent and a time to speak."

And it's true. During the holiday season there should be a time for exuberant and boisterous celebrating, and there should be a time for quiet reflections. There will be times to shout to the Lord, and there will be times to be still and know that He is God. In all of these times, may we be thankful and give praise to the One who gives us all things, even tears.

Give thanks in all circumstances, for this is God's will for you in Christ Jesus.
—I Thessalonians 5:18

CHAPTER ELEVEN

THE GLASS HALF-FULL

If you've ever taken one of those personality or temperament profile tests to determine if you're *sanguine, choleric, phlegmatic, or melancholy*, then you'll know what I mean when I say that I have a melancholy temperament. That does NOT mean that I'm sad all of the time or that I'm always singing the blues. Melancholies have some very good qualities and strengths—or so I'm told. However, we usually tend to see the negative side of anything first, be too critical, and expect too much from ourselves and others. We very often see the glass as half-empty rather than half-full. This melancholy trait in me puts a cloud over the part of me that should be thankful, and unfortunately, I'm not as thankful as I should be. I'm trying to change this by training myself to look for the good in every situation. It's not easy to change, though, when you're as good at complaining as I am. Yes, I've even been known to whine. There's a plaque in my home that says, "Thou shall not whine." I think that this should probably be the eleventh commandment–at least it should be for all of us who are of the melancholy persuasion.

I Thessalonians 5:18 says, "Give thanks IN all circumstances, for this is God's will for you in Christ Jesus." It's not always easy to obey this command. But I have found that many of the things about which I complain can actually also give me a reason to be thankful. If we look on the flip side of our complaints, we will usually find reasons for thanksgiving. We might gripe about the weather or the rain, but we know that we need the rain that causes flowers to grow. Even great pain brings forth great blessing–childbirth naturally comes to my mind here. Struggles and change cause us to grow. In pondering this season of Thanksgiving, I think about the reasons for my complaining and how I should really view these situations. Here are a few for starters:

I am so sick of doing laundry–the basket is always full. But I am thankful that I have a family who has plenty (and I do mean plenty!) of clothes to wear.

The kitchen is always full of dirty dishes, but I know I should be thankful that we always have plenty to eat. While there are those in the world who are starving, I am complaining that we are always eating.

I can't believe that my electricity bill is so high, but I am thankful that I stay cool in the summer and warm in the winter.

All I ever do is pay bills and try to "juggle" the money, but I'm thankful that we have bills to pay. So many in the world don't have any "bills" because they have no money and no possessions. Even the poorest among us is wealthy compared to the rest of the world.

Housework is never done, but I am thankful that I have a shelter over my head and furniture to dust and indoor plumbing to clean!

I am getting older, tired, and out of shape. However, I'm thankful that I am generally in good health. I don't ever spend any time in the doctor's office, so how can I complain when so many people are in hospitals?

I complain that there is nothing but trash on television and in movies, but I'm thankful that I don't have to watch. I'm thankful that there is an "off" button on every TV. I can choose what I watch and read. I need to remember what Psalm 101:3 says: "I will set no evil thing before mine eyes."

I bemoan the fact that the world is in a terrible shape and moral values seem to have vanished from the scene. Crime and violence are rampant; it's hard to feel safe any more. But I'm thankful that God is still in control, and my security is in Him, not in man or this world.

There are many more lists I could make, but you get the idea. Gratitude is an attitude, and it's an attitude I want to have. No matter what personality I have, no matter what season of the year or of my life it is, my prayer should be this–"Lord, give me an attitude of praise and thanksgiving, and let me see that glass as half-full. And, if you need to, remind me of that new commandment, *Thou shall not whine!* "

> *...You anoint my head with oil; my cup runs over.*
> —Psalm 23:5b (NKJV)

CHAPTER TWELVE

IT'S A WONDERFUL LIFE

The date on the calendar caught my attention. It was the first of November, and a feeling of panic began to rise up within me. No, I had not missed a birthday, anniversary, deadline, or anything else important. But I felt overwhelmed by the fact that I had done nothing yet to get ready for Christmas!! The world of advertising and retail (of which I was a part) was telling me that I was way behind–how could I be so slack?? In my stress-filled frame of mind I wondered how things got this way. Why does the world jump from pumpkins to presents, from spooks to Santa, from Halloween to Christmas? November is no longer a Thanksgiving month–it is a pre-Christmas month. I know that there is so much to do that we all feel the pinch to get started early, but why is there so much to do? I'm afraid we have all succumbed to the hype. We think that we have to have the perfect gifts, the perfect decorations, the perfect tree, the perfect food, etc.

On that first day of November I remembered something Pam Moore had said at our church's Women's Retreat in October. Pam had been the personal assistant and companion to Corrie ten Boom during the last years of Corrie's life. Sometimes when Pam was particularly stressed or distressed, Corrie would stop and pray, "Lord, help Pam to see great things great and small things small, that she might have a relaxed and happy life." And so, as I began to feel overwhelmed over the holidays, I prayed, "Lord, help me to see great things great and small things small." I tend to make small things great (you know–the "mountain out of a molehill" syndrome), and I many times overlook the great things as being great because I'm too busy looking at the small things. It just all boils down to changing our perspective and beginning to look at things from God's perspective. How does He see the things that we see as troublesome and annoying problems, huge in our eyes? How does He see the things that we don't even bother to give a passing glance? If we see things through the eyes of the world, we are seeing them through lenses that give a distorted view, and very probably a view that is the opposite of God's.

During that time I saw a greeting card that said, "It's a wonderful time *to know* that our hope rests in the ONE who never changes, *to trust* in the WORD that will endure forever, and *to abide* in the peace that only HE can give." That holiday season I decided that I wanted most of all to know, trust, and abide in Him. I determined that I would see the great things great and the small things small. I didn't want to sweat the small stuff or miss the great stuff...because I knew that with the right perspective, it really is *a wonderful life.*

> *I have come that they may have life, and that they may have it more abundantly.*
> —John 10:10 (NKJV)

CHAPTER THIRTEEN

NOT A FRUITCAKE, BUT A NUT

It's a well-documented fact by now. I'm just a little bit of a nut when it comes to Christmas. Well, okay. I'm a big nut when it comes to Christmas. I'm a little over-the-top. Well, okay. I'm a lot over-the-top. I have been known to embarrass my family with my enthusiasm over the holidays. It has become their Christmas tradition to make fun of me every year. They can all imitate my "oohs" and "aahs." (That's okay–let them mock. I saw what happened to Scrooge.) It's just that I personally don't think you can celebrate too much, decorate too much, have too many Christmas lights, listen to too much Christmas music, or watch too many Christmas movies. So, my children have just had to endure the pain of having friends over during the Christmas season who said in those surly teenage voices, "Uh…your mom really gets into this Christmas stuff, doesn't she?"

The thing some may not know is that I came by this naturally. I inherited it. My mother is an "over-the-top" Christmas celebrant, also. And her mother loved Christmas, too, and I'm sure it goes back much further than that. I can prove that I have a Christmas heritage, but, alas, I must give in to the fact that there are many who don't. Nor do they share my views. I hear many Christians talk about Christmas as if it is nothing but a pain in the neck. Oh, sure, it has been commercialized and cheapened by the world, but the world doesn't understand. They do not understand why we celebrate because they don't have Christmas in the place where it belongs–in the heart. Maybe we should try showing them why and how Christmas should be celebrated instead of complaining about the hype and the hoopla ourselves. If Christians are not excited about the message of Christmas, then there's something wrong. Maybe others don't celebrate as I do and want much less fanfare and decorating, and that's okay. But can we at least celebrate rather than complain? What is it that they say? Instead of cursing the darkness, let's light a candle.

So, go ahead, scoffers. Make fun of me all you want. Laugh at my lights, mock my merriment, disdain my decorations, chuckle at my clothes. But, just a word of warning–don't be surprised to find only a lump of coal in your stocking on Christmas morning!

*When they saw the star, they rejoiced with
exceedingly great joy.*
—Matthew 2:10 (NKJV)

CHAPTER FOURTEEN

MY CHRISTMAS HERITAGE

Those who know me well know that I **love** everything about Christmas. They may not know, however, that I inherited it. I have a "Christmas heritage." My mother grew up in a family of eight kids–she was somewhere in the middle. They had little money, but lots of love. Mom's mom was... well, I always thought she would make the perfect Mrs. Santa Claus. She was short and round, and she was jovial and fun-loving. She loved to sing–**really** sing. I guess if I had to conjure up a typical picture of Grandma Morris at Christmas, it would be a snapshot of her in the kitchen with her apron on, cooking and singing at the top of her lungs, "Oh, Beautiful Star of Bethlehem." Now Mom was a good child, always wanting to please, and always a giver. She has told us that she was given a little money for lunch at school, but for weeks before Christmas she wouldn't eat lunch. She would save her money so that she could buy Christmas gifts for her parents and all her siblings—no small feat. Through the years she has told us other wonderful stories about Christmas in her childhood. One year her dad surprised her with a doll he had seen her admire in a store window, even though it was one that he couldn't really afford. Christmas was just magical to her, but the most fun for her was giving gifts to others.

Well, I guess because of that background and that spirit, when she was grown and married and had five children of her own, she always wanted Christmas to be special. When all five of us reached school age, she began to work outside the home, and I suspected that her whole salary went to Christmas gifts for us. For her, less was not more; *more* was more. Quantity counted, and everyone's stack had to be the same. Even after we were all grown and married, she continued to have stacks of presents for all of us, our spouses, and our children. I knew by then that Mom must surely be working all year just for Christmas gifts. Mom and Dad's den floor would be covered with presents, and our marathon gift-opening ceremonies on Christmas Day would (and still do) take hours. Of course, we all have to open our gifts one at a time so that Mom can watch us.

I've begun to believe that in the last few years God has honored her Christmas spirit and given her a special Christmas blessing, you might say. First came the year that Dad had heart surgery and a leg amputation and was in the hospital for weeks, from September until early November. Those were dark days for all of us, but I could tell that Mom's light at the end of the tunnel was that he might be home before the holidays. I marveled that he was home and doing well enough before Thanksgiving that the holidays continued on as usual at Mom's house, and at Christmas the stacks of gifts were still there. Then just a couple of years later, in the early spring, Mom was diagnosed with cancer, and the long months of chemo and radiation and more radiation began. But by the late autumn months the treatments were over, and she began to feel a little better. Just the fact that she was no longer having treatments brightened her days and her outlook. And as she grew stronger, we had Thanksgiving as usual at her house, and of course, by that Christmas all of the usual traditions and hoopla were in place, and the shopping had all been done. Right after Christmas she bent over and "broke her back," to put it simply, because the bones in her lower back were so deteriorated from all of the treatments. She began a six-week period of complete bed rest. She was depressed, but knowing Mom, I knew that the disappointment she was feeling was not nearly as bad in January and February as it would have been before Christmas. I was so thankful for God's timing and His grace–through all of those difficult times, Christmas at Mom's house had remained the same.

So, as I said, I come by it naturally. I am a little crazy when it comes to Christmas, but it's my heritage. And my kids know that there are some things about Christmas that they can count on, no matter how far away they may roam. When they do come home, they know that they're not going to find one of those theme-decorated Christmas trees with all blue or all silver matching balls and bows. They know that we'll have the same eclectic tree with the same conglomeration of ornaments that stand for our memories through the years. They know that they will see the same ornaments and the same Advent calendar counting down the days 'til Christmas hanging in the same place that it has all of their lives. They know that the Snow Village will be in the den, and their stockings will still be hanging on the fireplace mantle; and there will still be a Christmas bedspread on my bed. And later when they come to visit me in the nursing home, they will know which room is mine because of all the Christmas decorations. There will be lights strung around my bed, and I'll be wearing my Christmas pajamas and watching endless hours of videos of my two little kids dancing around the Christmas tree. And if it's true that the elderly remember best the things from long ago, they just might hear me singing "Oh, Beautiful Star of Bethlehem." And if they listen closely, they just might hear Grandma Morris harmonizing with me from heaven and my Mom asking God if she can decorate heaven's Christmas tree.

The boundary lines have fallen for me in pleasant places; surely I have a delightful inheritance.
—Psalm 16:6

CHAPTER FIFTEEN

A NEW YEAR SCROOGE

I don't mean to be a New Year Scrooge…I really don't. I've just never been too fond of January. Oh, I wish I could be one of those optimistic people who love the idea of the fresh start, the new beginning, the blank new calendar pages. But I'm just not one of those people. For one thing, the new year signals the end of the holiday season, which totally depresses me. I am a certifiable Christmas nut (although I prefer to call myself "Mrs. Christmas Spirit"). I love everything about Christmas–even the things that many people don't like. As you can imagine, I absolutely dread the idea of having to put all Christmas things away. And even though I would NEVER do that as early as the first of January, that day does still remind me that the day of taking down Christmas is fast approaching. The holidays are officially over at that point, and by about the tenth day of January everyone begins to ask us why our outside Christmas lights are still on. A melancholy mood begins to overtake me right about the time the world is celebrating the new year. And the winter weather just seems to get a little drearier along with my mood.

For another thing, nothing makes me feel as old as a new year does. Where did last year go? I've always heard that time marches on, but that's not true. Time SPRINTS on. I'm not ready to turn the calendar. I was just beginning to get used to last year. But on the other hand, I'm not sure I'd want to be twenty-five again either. I'm confused–I'm not sure I'm ready for the new year; but I know that time must pass, things must change, life must go on. I certainly wouldn't want to go back and start all over! No wonder the new year confuses me. I'm just not ever sure I'm ready for the next step. I look back on the last year with nostalgia and remember the good times and the bad times, and I wonder what the new year will hold.

Thirdly, I don't really like resolutions. I have just enough fear of failure in me that I'm afraid to make resolutions. If I make them but don't accomplish them, then I have failed (at least in my own mind). Of course, every year I want to lose weight, read the Bible more, worry less, be a better person, spend more time with my family and with God, and slow down and savor the moments more often. I know that goals are admirable, but resolutions just add pressure to my life. What if I don't do them? What if I fail? Are those general desires really resolutions anyway? Are they specific enough, or are they too vague? The pressure mounts.

And so I sit here and stare at the blank new pages of my personal calendar and appointment book for the new year. Yes, they represent a fresh start, a new beginning, and new promise. But they don't really call out to me in an inviting sort of way or beckon to me to fill them in with new and exciting things. Last year's worn-out calendar makes me a little sad; but it's time to move on, start new things, learn to write a new year on my checks. After all, what is it they say–"out with the old, in with the new"? Who knows? This year may be the best yet. Maybe I will even make a few resolutions. Hey, I think I'll even go through this new calendar and begin to write in some things! Let's see…what is the earliest possible date next fall that I could get out my Christmas stuff……

My times are in Your hands….
—Psalm 31:15

FRIENDSHIP

CHAPTER SIXTEEN

THE STUFF OF LIFE

I've had a busy last few weeks. Yes, I was busy with work and the usual details of everyday life, but they were busy weeks in other ways, too. I had a reunion at my house of a women's Bible Study group from years past. My husband and I went away for a week-end with two young couples whose lives are quite different from ours because they still have young children.

One Thursday afternoon I said good-bye at the airport to good friends who were leaving for the mission field. Another week-end my husband and I took our daughter and three other high school girls to a concert in Dallas, and I think I am just beginning to get my hearing back. On another week-end I took the college girls in my Sunday School class to Branson. And on one Friday night in August we had a "going-away" party for and said good-bye to one of our long-time employees.

During these same weeks, I've been to a wedding, and I've been to a funeral. I've watched another "first day of school" come and go, and I had the inevitable "where did the years go" reflections of those school years when I had excited little ones with new crayons and lunch boxes. I can't possibly have a sophomore in college and a sophomore in high school, can I? But I do. I know—it sounds as if I'm about to burst into the chorus of "Sunrise, Sunset," doesn't it? I won't, but I have been thinking that all of the things I've mentioned above are the "stuff" of which life is made. There were reunions and good-byes, reflections and new starts, relationships and acquaintances, laughter and tears. They all remind me that the best things in life aren't "things." At least they are not "things" in the "possessions" sense of the word. And once again I wonder if I savor these intangible "things"—these special moments in time and these relationships with others—as I should. Or are there always stacks of unfinished work casting a shadow over my thoughts and long to-do lists cluttering the back of my mind? Are there images of unpaid bills and deadlines ever present, even when I should be giving someone my full attention?

We all need to be reminded that people and relationships need our full attention, particularly if we are busy parents. Children need our attention and the gift of our time, and the time spent with them should be savored—not rushed, not begrudged, not divided.

"One hundred years from now it will not matter what kind of house I lived in, how much money I had, or what kind of car I drove. But the world may be a little better because I was important in the life of a child." Making a difference in the life of another human being, child or adult, should be a goal for all of us because people and relationships are the "things" that make the memories of our lives. Moments with friends and those who touch our lives are the real "stuff" of which life is made.

If one falls down, his friend can help him up.
But pity the man who falls and has no one to
help him up!
—Ecclesiastes 4:10

CHAPTER SEVENTEEN

GOLD FRIENDS

I don't remember where I first heard it. I think my mother probably said it to me when I was a child–she knows all kinds of sayings like this one. "Make new friends, but keep the old. One is silver, the other gold." Now I understand better the validity of that little rhyme. I still like to make new friends, but I am especially happy that I have several really *old* friends. Now I don't mean that these friends are *old* in age, you understand, but they are friends that I've had almost my whole life. Several of us have been friends for over forty years, and when you're as "young" as we are, that's a long time!

I have often marveled at the fact that I still have a few precious friends who have remained close friends, even though busy lives and distance have separated us through the years. I have learned that the older you get, the more comforting it is to have people in your life who knew you when you were young. But I'm afraid it's rare today to have those kinds of friends, and it's becoming even more so in a society that's so mobile, so family fragmented, so "rootless," and sadly so often closed to friendships because of lack of time. I wonder if my children will ever even "stay in touch" with childhood friends when they grow older. We recently had a lesson in church that focused on the importance of cultivating and maintaining vital friendships. In Ecclesiastes 4:9-12 we read that "Two are better than one...if one falls down, his friend can help him up. But pity the man who falls and has no one to help him up!... Though one may be overpowered, two can defend themselves..."

Recently four of my old (I mean *gold*) friends (who all graduated from high school with me) and I went on an overnight trip with no agenda but to visit and catch up. We stayed up until 2:00 A.M. (difficult for our age!) just talking. We laughed until our sides hurt, and we shed a few tears as we shared some heartaches. Another old adage came to my mind: "Friendship doubles our joys and divides our sorrows." It's great to be able to share joys and sorrows with someone who "knew you when" but loves you anyway.

To be honest, I thought that we'd spend a lot of time reminiscing and that most of our conversations would start with, "Remember that time in junior high when we...?" But we did very little of that. We mostly talked about our lives now–our children, our challenges, and our changes as we turn the pages of the new chapters in our lives.

We don't all still live in our home town. Some of us previously lived out of state but now have moved back "home." But even those of us who do live here don't see each other that often. Maybe we see each other at an occasional ballgame or community function–but as with everyone, our lives are just too busy. It took months of planning to come up with a week-end that we could all manage to get away.

All five of us have parents who still live in our home town. Some of them (such as my parents) still live in the same houses where we had slumber parties when we were in junior high school. I don't know why, but that's somewhat comforting to me–I'm sure it's very rare. I guess in a world where everything changes so quickly, some consistency is comforting to all of us.

So, here's to you, my *old* friends, my *gold* friends…Criss, Becky, Beverly, and Patsy. Thanks for continuing to be a part of my life.

A friend loves at all times.
—Proverbs 17:17

CHAPTER EIGHTEEN

STRANDED: MIRACLES ON THE PINNACLE

New Year's Eve 1998 found us in our condo in Branson. Our friends, the Osborne family, had joined us to spend the night, and we planned to all return home late New Year's Day. The ten of us went out to a wonderful restaurant for dinner, came back to the condo, and rang in the New Year. After we found beds or sleeping bags for everyone, we finally settled down to sleep. But as we slept, the temperatures dropped and the sleet and freezing rain began to fall. We awakened to a winter wonderland of white–ice had covered almost everything.

Our condo is located in a resort a few miles out of Branson. Our particular condo building is called the Pinnacle–for good reason. It's located on the top of a hill. On New Year's morning Chuck, my husband, went out for a walk and told us that the resort's maintenance man was working hard to clear the roads. So, of course, armed with that information, the six of us who would rather shop than watch ballgames decided to go shopping. We planned to shop for a while and then bring back lunch for everyone since we had already devoured all of the breakfast and snack foods that we had in the condo. We were going to take our friends' big full-size van because our car would be crowded with six. Besides, all of the doors of our car were frozen closed. We did have to sit for some time in the van while enough ice thawed for us to see, but that didn't deter us. However, as we pulled out of the parking lot and sat at the top of the hill looking down a long ice-covered stretch of road, we were not so sure. If we slid any at all, we could just keep going at the bottom of the hill and go straight over the cliff across the road.

We finally decided not to try it but to go back instead, but we quickly found that backing up was not an option. As both Boyd and Debbie got out of the van to survey the situation, the other four of us just sat in the van and waited. Soon I realized that the van was beginning to move. Rosalind had noticed it about the same time, and we both yelled at the other two (Jeff and Bethany) to jump out. (My husband thinks it's hilarious that I was the only one who jumped out with my purse. My two younger fellow female jumpers left their purses in the van, and their husbands had to make a trip back to the van later to retrieve their purses. I told them as you get older your purse just becomes an extension of yourself.) As we were screaming and jumping out, Boyd turned to look. We all watched as the van seemingly in slow motion began to slide down the hill. In our minds' eyes, we all saw the usual TV vehicle crash–the van would inevitably go off the cliff, roll over several times, crash into a tree, and explode. I couldn't blame Boyd for his next words: "Well, there's something I don't want to watch." I felt so awful. We had invited his family to be our guests for a nice quiet New Year's holiday, and here he was–watching his family jump out of a moving vehicle and his van drive itself off a cliff. We did, however, all watch the van veer to the left, slowly go off the road, and then land in the trees off the side of the hill. Miraculously it did not roll over, and it did not crash. It was stopped by some large rocks and a tree that was just spindly and "giving" enough to bend with the weight of the van and stop it, rather than crush it. Of course, I'm not so sure but what there weren't a couple of angels holding up the van.

Sitting behind us watching all of this were three men in a four-wheel-drive truck. Two younger men were giving another man a ride into the Branson grocery store where he was a manager. They asked what they could do to help and told us the names of some tow services to call. We then gave them a fairly large amount of money and asked them to bring us back some groceries, since we were obviously stranded. We certainly didn't want to starve to death–after all, we had planned to leave that evening, so the food supply was running low.

The tow truck came before too long, pulled the van out, and took it up the next hill to the office area and level ground. The van had no damage, and it wasn't even scratched because of the thick layer of ice on it–the ice had protected it from the tree branches. The towing people charged even less than we thought it would cost and were on their way. We were all safe, and the van was not only drivable, but in remarkably good shape. *Miracle #1.*

After a good while, the young men had not come back with the groceries. My natural skepticism began to wonder if they would be back (since, after all, they had our money), but at just that time we saw their truck pull up. We went out to meet them, but they insisted on bringing the groceries in and unloading them on our counter. They had bought a wonderful variety of foods–breakfast foods, desserts, snacks, sandwich fixings, meat, etc. They also had the receipt and ALL of the change. As we insisted that they let us pay them for doing this for us, they said that they didn't want anything for their trouble. To us they were not just extremely helpful and polite young men–they were angels of mercy. *Miracle #2.*

Later that afternoon my husband decided to try to get our car out. The car did make it down the famous hill where the van had driven itself, but it could not make it up the next hill to the office. Chuck managed to turn the car around and head back up the first hill, but the car had to be pushed to make it back it up to the top. So, yes, we were indeed stranded. The poor maintenance men had tried to keep the resort's roads clear, but it was just a losing battle as the sleet continued to fall. We might as well accept it–we just couldn't leave.

That night we had a good meal, watched movies and TV, and played games. Everyone actually enjoyed the time together. There was never a harsh word spoken, and we realized that the ten of us truly did like each other. The close quarters were the proof of true friendship. *Miracle #3.*

The evening news reports on television continually mentioned power outages for thousands of people in the area. Several times our lights flickered, and we held our breaths. The condo is all electric with no fireplace, and the temperature was well below freezing. The thought of no heat was an unpleasant one, to say the least. But the electricity never went off, not even for a minute. *Miracle #4.*

Snow fell that evening, and the hills were even more beautiful the next day. Snow had covered all of the ice. Later that day we called the office and found that some of the roads were a little better. Once again Chuck tried to get our car out of the resort, and this time he was successful; so we decided to try to head for home.

It had been quite an exciting first day of the year. I personally had never spent New Year's Day, or any day for that matter, jumping out of a van that was moving. By the end of the first day of 1999 we had experienced several miracles. Sure, they might not be in the "parting of the Red Sea" category, but they were a manifestation of the kinds of miracles God does in our lives every day. It's just that we take them for granted. For example, there's the miracle of His protection and safe keeping of our lives and of our possessions. There's the miracle of neighborly kindness, sometimes even given to us by strangers. There's the miracle of true friendship and family–loving each other even in close quarters. The miracles of modern conveniences and electricity bring us comfort every day. And God allows us to see the miracle of the beauty of His creation (sometimes covered with snow) and reminds us that He controls the weather and the world.

I have to admit it–all in all, it wasn't a bad place to be stranded. We had a nice warm place to stay, TV's and VCR's, a washer and dryer, two bathrooms, and a full kitchen with plenty of food. As a matter of fact, as soon as I was back home where there was no beautiful snow and back at work and the hectic lifestyle that I led, I was just a little wishful that I could go back to the peace and quiet on the top of that hill–maybe I wasn't stranded long enough. But, Lord, just in case it ever happens again, could we please leave out that part where I have to jump out of a moving vehicle on an ice-covered hill?

Then all the multitude kept silent…. declaring
how many miracles and wonders God had
worked…
—Acts 15:12 (NKJV)

SEASONS OF LIFE

CHAPTER NINETEEN

DO I LOOK LIKE A HILLBILLY?

I love living in rural Arkansas. The road I live on had no name until recently. There was a small county road sign with a number on it, but nobody knew our road by that name. Everybody knew the road by the names of the people who live on that road. I grew up in a house (where my parents still live) less than a mile from my present home. Now our road has a name for 9-1-1 purposes, but I still doubt anyone knows the name of my road.

When we moved into our home we had decided to continue to just use our post office box in town that we used for our business for our home address as well. After all, we had to go to the post office every day to get our store's mail; why not just get our personal mail in the same box? This worked out fine and didn't seem to bother anybody for several years…until the time that it became unacceptable to have only a post office box for an address.

Every time I gave my address to anybody, they would tell me that I had to have a physical address. A post office box number was not enough. I tried to tell them that if they just printed my name and the name of my town on the envelope, everybody in town would know where to come get me. The people who were asking this were not just asking this for delivery purposes. No, they wanted to know my physical address everywhere that I wrote a check, everywhere that I filled out an application for credit for anything, everywhere that I filled out a form of any kind. The road on which I lived was not my address at the time. If we had received our mail at our home, our address at the time would have been some route or something. But we didn't receive our mail there, so it wasn't.

One summer my family and I were attending a convention in downtown Cincinnati, Ohio. While we were there I did some shopping in a large downtown department store. I found lots of end-of-the-season bargains. When I started to check out with my rather large purchase, the young salesgirl told me that if I would open a charge account with that particular store on that day I could get a discount on all of my purchases. She told me that the simple process would only take about five minutes with instant approval. Since that particular chain did not even have any stores in Arkansas, I knew there would be no temptation to use that card again. Since

I was buying several things, why not just go ahead and get that huge 10% discount and then never actually use the card? In my mind, the money saved would surely be worth the five minutes spent.

I didn't even have to fill out a form. The girl simply asked the necessary questions and entered the answers into the computer. Easy…until we got to the second question, the one right after "Name." "Address?"

Of course when I told her, she said, "No, I need your physical address. What's your house number?" I told her that I didn't have one, at which point she looked at me as if I were from outer space. "How can you not have a house number?" she asked. I explained that I lived in the country outside a small town in Arkansas, and none of us had house numbers. She plunged ahead and asked me for the name of my street. "I don't live on a street or a highway," I said. I explained that I lived on a dirt road. By this time she was flabbergasted (obviously this girl had never been out of inner-city Cincinnati, had never seen a house without a number, and had never seen a dirt road). She then looked at me with pity in her eyes and asked, "Do you have electricity?" "Yes," I said, "and indoor plumbing, too." She then called the person in accounting to give them my information for the instant approval, and she said on the phone (right in front of me), "You're never going to believe this–there's someone here from Arkansas who lives on a dirt road and doesn't even have a house number!!"

By this time I wasn't having fun any more. As a matter of fact, I was getting a little irritated. Did I look like a hillbilly or like I had just left Dogpatch? Did I have hayseed in my hair? Did I have straw in my teeth? Did I have the word *hick* stamped on my forehead?

Even though Jeff Foxworthy's definition of a redneck includes the phrase, "if the directions to your house start with the words 'turn off the paved road,'" I didn't and still don't consider myself or any of my neighbors hicks. And even though I didn't have a house number and my conversation was peppered with the word *ya'll*, I still didn't consider myself a hillbilly.

I did get my credit card and my discount in Cincinnati, though, and now I laugh every time I think of that young girl. I wasn't laughing a few days later, though, as we left Cincinnati. We left in our rental car in plenty of time to get to the airport and catch our plane. However, we did NOT allow enough time to take over an hour to drive ten miles. There was no accident or road construction—we were simply in rush-hour Friday afternoon traffic. Of course we had never taken into consideration the fact that thousands of people would be fleeing the city at the same time we were. As we rushed to our flight gate and tried to board, the person at the counter told us that the doors had already closed. We had missed our flight. I tried to explain to him that we were from rural Arkansas where we never have to worry about rush-hour traffic and that we just never thought about it, and on and on (as if that would get us on the plane). He just smiled at me in a condescending way as if to say, "You poor, pitiful hillbilly."

Oh, well, if being from a small town in Arkansas makes me a hick, then I guess I am one. But I have acres of land with beautiful trees that change color in the fall, friends and family just "down the road," and a house with all of the "modern" conveniences, including televisions, DVD and CD players, computers, and Internet. And city-dwellers, consider this–I NEVER have to worry about rush-hour traffic!!

Dwell in the land and enjoy safe pasture.
—Psalm 37:3

CHAPTER TWENTY

THE PAIN OF LETTING GO

It's spring now, and for a few months my husband and I have been visiting colleges with our daughter. CaraJean is a Senior this year, our youngest child, and our only daughter. She insists on going "away" to college. The closest one that she is considering is three hours away, and that is, of course, the one that I am rooting for (honestly, it really is an excellent college!).

The other day we were visiting this particular university, and my husband and I were in a parents' session where they showed a video of interviews with parents who had sent their children to this school. One woman described the close relationship she had with her daughter and the grieving process she went through during her daughter's entire senior year. She said she really thought she might need counseling when her daughter actually left home. "Finally!" I thought. "Someone truly understands how I feel." And I began to cry. I cried through that whole session, much to my husband's amusement. Then I cried at lunch that day when I told my daughter about it, and she, of course, sighed and rolled her eyes. Anyone living with a teenager has seen that expression.

I will miss my daughter, though, just as I have missed my son. The really remarkable thing is that I not only love them as my children, I *like* them as people. They, along with my husband, are my best friends and the people with whom I most enjoy spending time.

Letting go, it seems, is not an easy thing for any of us. These "letting go" experiences occur throughout our lives, in various areas and stages and degrees of intensity. You may be having to let go of a young child just starting to school, a child leaving home or getting married, or a parent whose age and illness mean that his or her time left here on this earth is short.

You may have to let go of expectations, desires, or possessions. It's so hard not to tighten our grip rather than hold loosely in our hand that which God has given us. We know in our intellect that everything is God's and that we are only given these people or things on a temporary loan. But in our hearts it's still hard to give them up, so we cling tightly, not wanting to open our hands and let go. Even in our crying and our stubbornness and our unwillingness, God understands. He had to let go, too, you know. His Son, the cross, the loss–the Easter season reminds us that God does understand the pain of letting go.

> *A time to weep and a time to laugh...a time to keep and a time to throw away.*
> —Ecclesiastes 3:4, 6

CHAPTER TWENTY-ONE

THE EMPTY NEST

The first day of school happened this year in my small town–just like always. But the first day of school won't ever be the same in my house again. There was no one here to get up to get ready for school. Our youngest child is there now, away at college, starting school without me to watch her go out the door. She's there now, living away from home for the first time, and I'm still here, living with an empty nest.

On her first day of classes, I called CaraJean to ask if she'd had someone take her "first day of school" picture as I had done for the past thirteen years. It's probably a good thing that I couldn't see the expression on her face when I asked. I can picture that look of total exasperation–she probably rolled her eyes.

Seasons come and seasons go. It's a new season of life for me as well as a new season of the year. Summer passed too quickly; I knew it would. We didn't travel much this summer, but we did take a family vacation to Florida at the beginning of the summer, in late May. It was a picture-perfect week, and I just today looked at a page from my travel journal. It read:

"I'm sitting in a comfortable lounge chair right at the ocean's edge. The wind is blowing; it's comfortable, not hot. The sun is still shining, though it's after 6 P.M. Few people (very few!) are left on the beach–mostly young families playing in the sand. I'm reading, and writing, and wishing I could stay here forever. But then again, I guess if I did, it would not always seem this special. Sadly, we all have a way of making the daily routine mundane, no matter what it is. It is the fact that these brief interludes of sand and beach in our land-locked lives are so rare that makes them so magical. Water lapping at the shore is a sound that is exotic, soothing, romantic, and foreign to our everyday existence. It seems almost a pity that it is so far away from our daily lives. But for those of us who travel to the shore occasionally, it is a simple symphony to our tired ears, a balm to our weary souls."

But now it's autumn, and those of us who live in Arkansas may find a symphony in the rustle of fall leaves or a balm in the beauty of a brilliantly hued tree. There is a catch, though–we must take the time to listen and look. We may have to actually stop our busy lives and "sit a spell" on our front porches. But I'm reasonably sure that if we do, we'll realize that no days should be considered mundane or taken for granted. In the quiet we will understand that seasons come and seasons go, vacations become memories, and children grow up and leave home. And that is how it's supposed to be.

> *There is a time for everything and a season for every activity under heaven.*
> —Ecclesiastes 3:1

CHAPTER TWENTY-TWO

A TEMPORARY RESIDENCE

It's no longer the days that are flying by; it is now the seasons that are fleeting. I know I shouldn't be surprised by the speed at which life travels. The Bible clearly tells us to expect it. "Lord, remind me how brief my time on earth will be. Remind me that my days are numbered, and that my life is fleeing away." (Psalm 34:9 NLT) Pretty plain, isn't it? In Rick Warren's book *The Purpose Driven Life* he reminds us that life is a temporary assignment. "Realizing that life is just a temporary assignment should radically alter your values. Eternal values, not temporal ones, should become the deciding factors for your decisions." Seeing life through God's view and having an eternal perspective on life should change the way we live. It *should.* But our vision clouds and our focus blurs when we forget that "this world is not my home and I'm just a'passing through," as the old song says. We get too attached to our temporary residence.

During the few days surrounding the funeral of my husband's father, my husband and I felt a strong sense of that eternal perspective on life. Nothing of this world mattered–not work, or business, or to-do lists, or petty everyday tasks and problems. These things were set aside; they could wait. We spent time with family members we hadn't seen much; we shared memories; we cried with friends who came to visit; we hugged our children tightly and reminded them often how much their grandfather loved them. We talked about the peace and comfort we have in knowing what happens after this life is over.

But after those days, we all went back to work and life as usual, and it was important to do that, of course. However, I noticed how quickly we are pulled back into a "here-and-now" perspective rather than an eternal one. The world is "too much with us," I'm afraid. We are so busy, so wrapped up in those attachments, and so tired from running on the treadmill of life that it's hard to think with a clear perspective. Of course, we need to live fully in this life and do as much good on earth as we possibly can, and therein lies the challenge for most of us, I guess. We need to live as fully and completely as we can in this life, with purpose, but we must do so without losing an eternal perspective. Again, Rick Warren says, "When you fully comprehend that there is more to life than just here and now, and you realize that life is just preparation for eternity, you will begin to live differently. You will start *living in light of eternity*, and that will color how you handle every relationship, task, and circumstance."

Remembering what's important in the light of eternity helps us to not major on the minors, sweat the small stuff, or fret over evildoers. And that, after all, is really good news.

> *…you are a mist that appears for a little while and then vanishes.*
> —James 4:14b

TRAVEL

CHAPTER TWENTY-THREE

EXPECTING THE GOOD

Sometimes I think about how much attention and credit we give to the evil forces of this world. Of course they exist, and we should be alert and prepared to do battle, for our "enemy the devil prowls around like a roaring lion." But maybe we should dwell a little more than we do on the "good"–the "whatsoever things." "Whatsoever things are true, whatsoever things are honest, whatsoever things are just, whatsoever things are pure, whatsoever things are lovely, whatsoever things are of good report… think on these things" Philippians 4:8. Maybe we should get a little more excited about the fantastic things that God is doing in the world today! We very often expect the worst from people, probably because we have been conditioned to do so. We are so often surprised by kindness, goodness, and honesty that we almost dismiss them.

I remember the first time that my family and I had the opportunity to visit New York City. We stayed downtown, right on Times Square, and frankly, I was prepared to be scared. I expected (because of stereotypes) that the citizens of New York City would be rude, abrupt, and unfriendly. I was shocked to find that some of them were actually quite nice, even from my Southern hospitality standard's perspective. The streets were extremely busy, of course (it was only a few days before Christmas). Once in the hustle and bustle of the foot traffic on the sidewalks, I saw a woman trip over the curb and fall to the pavement. My first reaction was to panic because I was sure that people would just trample over her as they hurried on by. But before I could react, several people had stopped to help her up. Later, to my surprise, more than one smartly-dressed New York businesswoman in Starbucks complimented me on the Christmas sweater that I was wearing. (Of course, I realize that all of these women dressed in sleek black from head to toe had probably never seen a Christmas sweater with quite as much color as mine had!) Anyway, I know that I was pleasantly surprised on more than one occasion. Sure, I encountered some rude salesclerks, but I'll bet there were some of them in Arkansas, too, at that time of the year. And we did see some people on the streets who, to be perfectly honest, were downright scary-looking. But I need to remind myself often that all of these people are just human beings whom God loves just as much as He loves me.

So I'm going to try to **not** be surprised by the good things I hear about people and to **not** be surprised when people, even in unlikely places, turn out to be good and decent. I'm going to look for evidence of the increase in good, not just the increase in evil. Maybe we should do as our mothers always said, "If you can't say anything nice, just don't say anything at all." In our conversations and our messages and our opinions of people, let's try to say something nice for a change.

I'm still confident of this: I will see the goodness of the Lord in the land of the living.
—Psalm 27:13

CHAPTER TWENTY-FOUR

A HELICOPTER PRAYER

Palm trees. Ocean breezes. Sand and sunshine. It was a dream come true–a Hawaiian vacation on the beautiful garden island of Kauai. We were celebrating our twenty-fifth wedding anniversary. It was a perfect paradise worthy of such a tremendous milestone in our lives.

There were advertisements everywhere, though, warning us that the ONLY way to truly see this small island was from a helicopter. After all, only the coastal areas were populated and had a road system–the interior of the island was inaccessible because of the jungles and mountainous terrain. I knew that my husband would absolutely love to take a helicopter ride but that he wouldn't do it if I didn't. So I pretended that I **really** wanted to take a helicopter ride to see the island. Of course he took me up on it. And well, we all do crazy things to make the one we love happy, I guess–especially in a tropical paradise.

I reasoned that it couldn't be that bad. After all, I don't mind flying in an airplane at all. I actually prefer flying to driving on any trips, so I fly fairly often. I guess I just feel protected by the huge airplane. I can even get up and walk around in a plane. Normally, I pray for the plane and the pilot at the beginning of the flight; then I settle in, become absorbed in something good to read, and don't even really think about being in the air, unless there's a problem. On occasion I have even calmed scared passengers sitting beside me.

On the other hand, I don't like to stand near the cliff of a mountain (nor do I want my family members to do so). I don't climb to the top of the look-out towers to look out. I don't lean over the balcony of a hotel room on a high floor to see the view below. In short, I guess I'm afraid of heights, but this really didn't register in the helicopter decision. Surely it would be similar to being in a plane, right? I couldn't have been more wrong.

I assumed I would sit beside Chuck, between him and someone else, and I could hang on to him or lean on his shoulder and not look if things were too scary. Little did I know that we would be assigned seats–by weight, no less!! I should have known better than to do anything where the first thing they ask is your weight–not a good sign. Chuck sat in the front with our pilot (who was flying barefoot because he had a surfing accident–another less-than-comforting sign). I sat in the back by the door with a young honeymoon couple on my right, rounding out the five passengers who, as crowded as it was, looked like too many to me. "Sitting by the door" is an understatement. There was no armrest, no space, no protection, nothing to hang on to–just a thin little door with an open plastic window. So there I was, higher than the mountains, literally sitting on the edge, and I'm afraid of heights. What WAS I thinking?!?! Of course, I assumed that my door would probably malfunction and open, and I would naturally fall out because my seat belt could not hold me as the wind sucked me out into the wild blue yonder. I know the young girl sitting beside me was wondering why I seemed to be trying to sit in her lap! As we soared above mountaintops and dipped into valleys (thankfully I never get any kind of motion sickness) and flew out over the ocean, I kept my eyes closed and kept telling myself I could stand anything for an hour, couldn't I? After all, Philippians 4:13 was still true, wasn't it?

I opened my eyes and saw Chuck having the time of his life beside the surfer dude. He was literally beaming and shaking his head in amazement. I have to admit–the scenery below us was beautiful. The mountains, the waterfalls, the coastline–they were breathtaking, but inside I was still shaking. I dug my fingernails into my legs (there was nothing else to grasp) and prayed the prayer. You know the one. "Lord, if you'll just get me out of this situation safely, I **promise** I'll never do anything foolish like this again." Whenever Chuck looked back at me (we couldn't communicate because of the noise) I just tried to smile a brave smile. He was so happy—I was just grateful that I didn't have to ruin his fun by screaming or throwing up or something. Bless his heart—I think he thought I was having a good time.

After we landed safely (thank you, Lord) Chuck said, "Now, see, that wasn't so bad, was it? Now that you've done it and survived, you could do it again, couldn't you?" Yeah. Right. And break a vow to God? I don't think so.

> *It is better not to vow than to make a vow*
> *and not fulfill it.*
> —Ecclesiastes 5:5

CHAPTER TWENTY-FIVE

THE OLDER, THE BETTER

I just returned from a trip I have wanted to take almost all of my life. I wish you could have been there with me. Well, no, I don't guess I really do because then I wouldn't have been traveling light, which is always a goal of mine although never attained.

My husband and I took a trip to New England to see the fall foliage. We stayed in Vermont but drove through other states as well in our quest to see as many leaves as we possibly could. The color was magnificent, and we were not disappointed. The creative and colorful handiwork of God is so evident during the autumn season. The mountains and the streams were so picturesque that I could barely pass a scene without taking a picture. During our short five days there, we took a carriage ride in Montreal,

Canada, rode a train through the White Mountains of New Hampshire, drove to the Maine coast and took pictures of lighthouses, rode a ski gondola to the top of the highest mountain in Vermont (where it was snowing), and drove countless hours simply taking in the scenery of Vermont's Green Mountains and other areas.

The villages in Vermont are just what I had expected them to be–quaint, beautiful, full of history, uncluttered, and simple. Every village has a white church with a tall steeple spire, a general store, and maybe a town hall or meeting place and an occasional small gas station. However, no small villages have convenience stores or fast food restaurants (or chains of any kind). The population size is not listed under the names of the towns on the entrance signs, but the signs do list the year of establishment, most often a late 1700's date. Obviously the size is not important at all, but the age and the history are. Specifically, the older, the better–it seems almost a contrast to the American philosophy we see in today's culture where "young" and "new" are most often preferred. Within those quiet villages is a reverent respect for the old buildings, the historic sites, and the simplicity of life. The people understand what makes their small villages so special. Vermont's former governor once said that one of Vermont's special traits is in knowing "where our towns begin and end." It seems a simple concept, but it shows the importance of the identity of each small town. None of them will be swallowed up by the "progress" of expansion that sometimes begins to run towns together in large metropolitan areas.

Okay, I confess–I do like big cities, I love malls, and I've always bought "new" rather than "antiques." But I have a new respect for the simple beauty of covered bridges and farmhouses. Now that I'm old enough that I appreciate age (and want others to do the same), I just may learn to appreciate the simple and serene as well–an idea that's sure to be tested in the hustle and bustle of my life.

> *...and the splendor of old men is their gray head.*
> —Proverbs 20:29 (NKJV)

CHAPTER TWENTY-SIX

TRAVELING LIGHT

It's the middle of July, and I've noticed something. Almost everyone I know is either about to leave for vacation, is currently on vacation, or has just returned from vacation. There's a whole lot of packing going on. Since I fit into none of those categories, I am just a little envious because I love to travel. I love to plan, and I love to pack to go somewhere because the anticipation is probably the best part. However, I have never really learned to travel light. The last time I returned from a trip I realized that I had not worn even half of the clothes or shoes that I had packed. I always pack for "what if" situations. I pack clothes for every possible need by saying "what if I need this" or "what if I need that." After packing all those clothes, I look at each outfit and think that if I do wear that one, then I'll need the appropriate shoes, purse, and jewelry. I know, I know–many people do not understand this, but some of you women know exactly what I mean.

I am determined, however, to learn to travel light. My goal is to someday leave for a trip with one small bag and yet upon arrival never once regret that I didn't bring something. It is a far-fetched dream right now, but I will achieve it–as I said, I am determined to succeed. Thinking about literally traveling light made me realize that I also want to learn to symbolically travel light in life as well. I live life on a "what if" basis way too often. I carry bags that weigh me down with "what ifs" like worry, fear, and anxiety. I wear myself out sometimes with the weight of baggage that I don't need to carry. Jesus said that His yoke is easy and His burden light; He invites us to come to Him with our burdens and He will give us rest. He will carry that heavy luggage when we can't. Why do we humans continue to struggle with burdens we were never meant to carry? Why do I have to consider every "what if" and pack them in my luggage, struggle to drag them through life, and then realize that they didn't even matter or maybe never even occurred? Just like those extra clothes in my suitcase, they were never even worn or needed.

In thinking on these things I looked for a Max Lucado book on my bookshelf that addresses this very topic, and there it was–*Traveling Light*. Imagine that? This excellent book tackles the loads that we all lug but were never intended to carry, such as fear, worry, and discontent. Using the twenty-third Psalm as a guide, Lucado shows us how to trust God with our burdens, to set our baggage down at His feet, and to learn to travel a little lighter. In his words, "For the sake of those you love, travel light. For the sake of the God you serve, travel light. For the sake of your own joy, travel light."

I'm ready now. I can't wait for my next trip, whenever it will be. If you see me leaving for vacation, you'll be amazed that I have only one small bag on my arm. But ask me if I've left the luggage of life not just at home because I'm on vacation, but at the Father's feet every day. Then, and only then, will I truly be *traveling light*.

> *Take no bag for the journey, or extra tunic, or*
> *sandals or a staff.*
> —Matthew 10:10

EPILOGUE

JUNE 2007

As I'm sure you could tell, these pages were written over about a ten-year period of my life. Many, many changes took place in that particular period of my life, as they do with everyone. Ten years ago I had two extremely busy teenagers who caused **me** to lead an extremely busy life. I had a husband who was building his business and working extra-long hours, and I was trying to help him with that. Today those teens are grown-up adults living in other places with such busy lives of their own that I just hope for a phone call now and then. Ten years ago I was actively, hands-on involved in their lives–now I watch them from afar juggle their own lives and call me whenever they can to give me an update. We sold that business that so consumed our lives and now my husband, Chuck, is a relief pharmacist working for other worn-out business owners when they need days off or take vacations. Ten years ago I was going to ballgames (lots of ballgames!), school programs, and trying my best to keep up with all of my children's activities. I was writing the paychecks of those who worked for us, handling personnel, interviewing employees, and going to gift markets to buy the gifts we sold. Now I spend most of my days alone, either reading or sitting in front of a computer, thinking, writing, and contemplating how my computer knows so much. I am enjoying the changes, but then again, there's a sadness as well. Our pharmacy was sold again a year after we sold, and now it's gone out of business. It's sad to drive by that building. We are "out of the loop" in our small community because we're just not in town as much. We once saw hundreds of people that we knew come through the doors of our store every week. Now I might see someone I know at the occasional trek to the post office. And, yes, that's sad. The winds of change have blown hard in the last few years, but that is the stuff of which our lives are made. So, now I'm trying to anticipate what things I'll be able to write about next. I'm excited to report as I finish this book that we will soon be first-time grandparents! Imagine that! I can just feel a wealth of new material for the next book coming my way. I don't know what else might be on the horizon, but I can promise you this: I'll always be looking for a new view...so please stay tuned. God bless.

ENDNOTES

CHAPTER 22

1. Rick Warren, *The Purpose Driven Life* (Zondervan, 2002), 50.
2. Rick Warren, *The Purpose Driven Life* (Zondervan, 2002), 37.

CHAPTER 26

1. Max Lucado, *Traveling Light* (Thomas Nelson, Inc., 2001), 8.